Debt

By the same author
Saving

Idea & Concept: **Juliane Otterbach**
Text: **Joly Braime**
Psychology Chapter: **Monika Heller**
Illustration: **Flora Douville**

Commissioning Editor: **Georgina Laycock**
Production: **Otterbach & Partners Ltd**
Design: *Dear Dad,* **Matthias Megyeri**
Editor: **Lucinda Hawksley**
Editorial Assistant: **Kira Hesser**
Consulting Editors: **Caroline Blake**, **Anthony Pearson**

Juliane Otterbach

Debt

ALLEN LANE
an imprint of
PENGUIN BOOKS

ALLEN LANE

Published by the Penguin Group
Penguin Books Ltd, 80 Strand, London WC2R 0RL, England
Penguin Group (USA) Inc., 375 Hudson Street, New York, New York 10014, USA
Penguin Group (Canada), 90 Eglinton Avenue East, Suite 700, Toronto,
Ontario, Canada M4P 2Y3 (a division of Pearson Penguin Canada Inc.)
Penguin Ireland, 25 St Stephen's Green, Dublin 2, Ireland
(a division of Penguin Books Ltd)
Penguin Group (Australia), 250 Camberwell Road, Camberwell,
Victoria 3124, Australia (a division of Pearson Australia Group Pty Ltd)
Penguin Books India Pvt Ltd, 11 Community Centre,
Panchsheel Park, New Delhi – 110 017, India
Penguin Group (NZ), 67 Apollo Drive, Rosedale, North Shore 0632, New Zealand
(a division of Pearson New Zealand Ltd)
Penguin Books (South Africa) (Pty) Ltd, 24 Sturdee Avenue,
Rosebank, Johannesburg 2196, South Africa

Penguin Books Ltd, Registered Offices: 80 Strand, London WC2R 0RL, England

www.penguin.com

First published 2008
1

Copyright © Juliane Otterbach, 2008

The moral right of the author has been asserted

Set in Corporate E
Printed in Italy by Graphicom, srl

A CIP catalogue record for this book is available from the British Library

ISBN: 978–1–846–14053–2

Legal Disclaimer
We want to empower people to get an overview of their finances and learn about
the options they have. However, this book is in no way meant to replace a financial
adviser. We strongly recommend that you seek the opinion of an independent
financial adviser who understands your particular circumstances before embarking
on drastically new strategies with your finances. As publisher Penguin cannot
accept liability for any loss which you may suffer as a result of following the
suggestions contained in this book.
All website links set out in this book were correct at the time of going to press.
The author and the publisher cannot take any responsibility for content appearing
on third party websites.

Contents

Introduction

How many unopened bank statements are you hiding right now? Is your wardrobe brimming with designer labels you can't afford? Do you know the APRs on all your credit cards? Fact is, pretty much everyone lives beyond their means. The trouble is that sometimes it feels like our generation is already fighting a losing battle, so there's no point fighting it.

The way the world seems to work is that we live hand to mouth for a few years, our spending exceeding our income, borrowing the difference from an endless number of companies, all desperate to lure us into debt. The temptation is to carry on like this, because as long as we're getting by and there's enough to pay the bar tab and the rent then that's all that matters, right? Bury your head in the sand. Rack up a cocktail tab on your card. Would you like an advice slip with your cash? No bloody way.

The thing is that living in debt can cost you a ridiculous amount of cash on top of what you borrow and, what's more, it's self-perpetuating. The worse your previous record is, the more interest people can get away with charging you on new loans, and so it rattles on. You already give more than enough of your hard-earned cash to the tax man without carving out another fat slice for a bunch of guys at a bank, and by rights, you owe it to yourself to figure out how to get that interest back into your pocket.

Obviously, if you could have paid it all back easily, then you would have done it years ago. We're not here to preach; we've been there. We want to talk about finances in the way we would like to read about them.

We want to show you easy ways to dig yourself back up into the daylight. Knowledge is power. There is no reason to be scared of sorting out your finances. There are no quick fixes, but it's worth a bit of hassle to finally get on top of something that could crush you for a very long time. And, once you're back on an even keel, you can take your new-found riches and start investing them, because making money is self-perpetuating too.

Spending Behaviour

'Years ago a person, he was unhappy, he didn't know what to do with himself – he'd go to church, start a revolution – something. Today you are unhappy? Can't figure it out? What is the salvation? Go shopping.'

Arthur Miller

Ever since the first caveman decided to barter stones for a share of his neighbour's hunting spoils, the whole race has been dependent on shopping. Even those who hate to shop have to do so regularly, in order to eat. What started out as a simple practical function, has become a way of life. We are surrounded by shopping malls – some the size of a small village – shopping streets, online shops, mail-order catalogues and entire TV channels devoted to shopping. All these things make consumption on a grand scale as easy as possible. For some, shopping is a chore they have to force themselves to do. For others it's a highly pleasurable activity and the perfect way to spend free time.

Symbolic Consumption

So, why is shopping perceived as rewarding and why do we buy so many things we don't need? Many of us have trouble fitting all our clothes in the wardrobe, yet we still feel compelled to buy more. Psychologists and sociologists talk about 'symbolic consumption' – the fact that people often define themselves by the things that they buy. If that is so, shopping stops being about the acquisition of things and becomes the buying of identity. By buying and consuming objects we can shape the image of how we see ourselves – and how we are seen by others.

Clothes, for example, have a high symbolic value, not least because they are on public display all the time. What a person wears is often indicative of what kind of music they like, what kind of home they live in, what kind of friends they have, even what kind of job they do. By wearing specific clothes, people place themselves in a particular sphere. Symbolic consumption is not only about clothes, however, it is also about the food you eat, the type of bar you go to, even what kind of holiday you take. Something as simple as buying a drink can be a symbolic act: do you go to the nearest shop to get your lunchtime juice because it's easier, or do you go out of your way to visit a local fair-trade smoothie bar?

In order for consumer products and brands to function as communication symbols, their meanings must be socially shared. Thanks to advertising and the media, most people have a fairly good understanding of individual brands and those brands' personalities.

Aspirational Shopping

Shopping not only influences who someone is, but also what they would like to become. Marketers often talk about 'aspirational shopping', especially when it comes to luxury products. Top fashion designers are business savvy – they know that many people aspire to the lifestyle their designs appear to offer, but that their humble wallets won't stretch to buying them. As a result, designers make the most of their profits from much more affordable 'signature' accessories, such as sunglasses, scarves, perfume and cosmetics.

It's not only the goods themselves you're buying – even the bags your purchases come in play an important role in the psychology of shopping. People will proudly reuse a designer carrier bag again and again, but a carrier bag from a less salubrious shop is quickly turned into a bin liner.

Shopping As Therapy

The expression 'retail therapy' is everywhere. It's become a buzzword for advertisers, evoking overtones of groups of friends enjoying long, happy lunches surrounded by bulging shopping bags. Psychologists refer to it as 'compensatory consumption' – an expression which, strangely enough, hasn't yet caught on in the advertising industry.

Yet can shopping really make you feel better? According to research, it can. Buying yourself a little present can actually help lighten your mood, although this is usually temporary. If your spending is excessive and unreasonable, the resultant high will be followed by negative feelings of guilt, shame, fear and anxiety. It rapidly becomes a vicious cycle as shoppers then try to recreate the initial high by buying something else to cheer themselves up, with the negative feelings promptly following on again and so on ...

Excessive and Compulsive Spending

It has become common for people to proudly describe themselves as 'born to shop' or a 'shopaholic', yet there are some for whom the idea of being addicted to shopping is a genuine condition. The need for 'retail therapy' is a much stronger impulse in excessive or compulsive buyers.

It's no joke: compulsive buying has been classified as a psychiatric disorder. It is identified as an urge to spend that is so overwhelming the person is unable to control it. Compulsive buying disorder is said to affect up to 10 per cent of adults in Western developed countries, with 70–80 per cent of those being young women.

Many compulsive buyers also suffer from other self-control disorders including gambling addiction, eating disorders and severe mood swings. Medical studies of compulsive buyers have identified that they tend to have fewer dopamine receptors, thus giving them a need to seek vicarious thrills. Unlike other thrillseekers, compulsive buyers don't decide to run marathons, backpack around the world or throw themselves off tall bridges with bungee ropes tied to their ankles; instead they seek the instant gratification of shopping – making purchases that they believe, in that initial moment, will make them more beautiful, successful or happy.

Psychologists have related compulsive buying to a need to escape: most usually trying to escape one's own self. Typically these people set extremely high standards for themselves that they are unable to meet. This in turn leads to a feeling of failure, anxiety and depression. When these negative feelings become too strong they try to block them out by focusing on a very low-level task like shopping. The long-term consequences such as debt are overridden by the need to feel instantly better about oneself.

A milder form of the disorder is known as excessive buying. This is far more commonplace and, as long as the person has enough money to pay for their spending habit, society does not even view it as a problem. You know you're in trouble when:

- shopping boosts your mood initially, but later leaves you feeling anxious, guilty or depressed
- you often feel compelled to buy things you don't need and/or can't afford
- some purchases are never used (and some even have the price tag still attached)
- you hide or lie about purchases to others

How Would You Like to Pay?

In the twenty-first century there are so many ways to spend money: credit cards, debit cards, store cards and cheques as well as cash and direct debit. We can spend it online, in shops, over the phone. We can buy goods from the other side of the world and have them shipped to us without even leaving our sofas.

Since the 1980s researchers have been comparing consumers who pay by credit card and those who use cash or cheques. People paying by credit card are willing to pay more than double the price for the same item than consumers paying by cash. They also make more instant decisions to buy something, rather than taking the time to think it over. Today, larger numbers of people than ever before pay by card for everything – and those are the people who tend to overspend. Those who use cash are much cannier at keeping within their budgets.

It seems that paying by card doesn't immediately sink into the consumer's brain; it lets them spend as if the purchase hadn't actually been made, and that can seriously mess up mental accounting. People paying by card simply do not visualize the amount as well as they would do if they had to hand over hard cash. Paying by credit card relieves some of the pain associated with spending money, as it's more abstract and payment is not immediate. It's even been proved that different parts of the brain start functioning when you're buying something with a credit card as opposed to with cash. It's all a question of the pleasure/pain principle. People tend to automatically balance the immediate pleasure derived from possessing an object against the pain of paying for it: the thrill of getting something new overshadowing the sensible voice of reason. It's a bit like buying a double espresso and fixating solely on the expected pleasure you'll be deriving from the caffeine hit, ignoring the 'pain' involved in paying a ridiculously inflated price for half a tiny cup of beans soaked in water.

Mental Accounting

Mental accounting is a form of bookkeeping that everybody does more or less automatically, although not necessarily consciously. Studies have shown that we divide our finances between separate mental accounts, such as going out, household expenses, clothes, buying birthday presents etc., and then keep a mental tally of how much we have left to spend. For instance, it's a common January phenomenon that people stop going out in order to 'pay off' Christmas; that's when the brain starts working out a new budget to try and make up for the previous month's binge-ing. For many people, self-control allows them to stay within their mental budget; for example, they might go for a couple of expensive nights out straight after payday, but then they spend the last week of the month staying in to compensate.

The problem with mental accounting is that it is so difficult to do accurately that we often cheat, allowing for a little 'creative bookkeeping' or convincing ourselves that we are buying less than we are. Mark Twain supplied a perfect example of this in 1897: having limited himself to one cigar a day, he started shopping for bigger and bigger cigars until he found one of such proportions that he 'could have used it as a crutch'.

Spending As Saving

Throughout 1998, anthropologist Daniel Miller studied the shopping behaviour of the residents of a street in North London. His major discovery was that, for most people, the most important factor in shopping is actually saving – but this did not mean they were spending less money. Think about how many times you've heard someone say, 'I saved £5 on this in the sale' rather than, 'This cost me £10'. By classifying spending as saving we justify a lot of expenses, both to others and to ourselves.

Shops have worked this one out for themselves. There are no longer simply the classic summer and winter sales; now shops hold regular mid-season, end-of-season and out-of-season sales. Most consumers mistakenly believe this will save them money, but shops hold sales for a reason: to get their mitts on even more of your money. They know shoppers are so easily tempted by 'bargains' they tend to ignore the fact that they are buying something they would never have bought if it hadn't been on sale. Shops also use other strategies such as 'buy one get one free' to lure people into buying products they wouldn't have thought of buying otherwise, but which they can now happily classify as a bargain.

Tips to Avoid Overspending

Limit impulse purchases: Unnecessary spending often occurs on the spur of the moment. You walk into a shop, see something and feel you just can't leave without it, even though you didn't know it existed 10 minutes earlier. Sound familiar?

To prevent this, make a list before you set out. Write down the things you need and try to stick to it. If you know you're a regular impulse buyer, have a long honest think about your spending pattern. When is it that you splurge money? When you're sad? When you're feeling stressed? If so, try to avoid shopping in these situations and consider cheaper actions to repair your mood, such as exercise (clinically proven to help reduce mild depression) or going to the cinema instead of buying an expensive new outfit.

Track expenses: Most of us are not good mental bookkeepers, mainly because it's difficult to keep track of how much money we spend and on what. If you're forever wondering what happened to that extra £20 you were sure was in your wallet, start writing down every penny you spend during the course of a day – every newspaper, every chocolate bar, even that handful of change you gave to a busker. Most people are stunned when they realize how much they habitually spend on insignificant things.

Setting realistic goals: If you've ever tried to go on a diet, it's likely that, as soon as you started, all you could think of was food. In a similar way, simply telling yourself not to think about shopping or spending money won't help – but setting realistic goals might. Nothing is more frustrating than constantly underachieving one's goals, so avoid all-or-nothing ultimatums, or your angry inner being will start to rebel. Try restricting how often you go shopping, i.e. one weekend in three instead of every Saturday and Sunday, and ask your friends to help you do other fun things in your spare time, to take your mind off it.

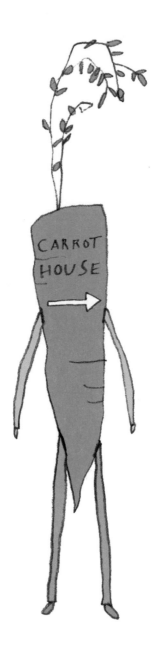

Student Life

It's a pricey business, university. Beyond the cost of getting educated, there are a-million-and-one extra expenses: rent, books, extravagant foaming hot chocolates, to name but a few.

For better or worse, you'll never be short of someone to give you a loan. Where thrifty housewives in their forties struggle to get a credit card, students are frequently lured into borrowing huge amounts of cash. As a young person with prospects (you hope) and massive potential to default on your payments in the early years, **everyone wants your debt**.

You will need to find approximately £10,000 to finance a year at college, including tuition fees of up to £3,070. Rent varies depending on where you study, and what kind of hellhole you're prepared to put up with, but expect to pay between £40 and £100 a week – and that's just for a room; you'll have to pay a lot more to get your own front door. Bills and food knock this weekly tab up by another £35–£45, and the NUS reckons the average student spends around £100 a month on going out.

The Student Loans Company

Of all the people who'll lend you money, these guys give you the sweetest deal of all. The Student Loans Company is a public sector body that gives government-funded loans to students – and that means really low interest rates. The interest is charged at the current rate of inflation (based on a yardstick called the Retail Prices Index), and is adjusted every year. This means that the amount you pay back is the same in real terms – which means it's adjusted to match inflation – as the amount you borrowed. You won't get a deal like that anywhere else.

Most student loans come in two parts; one for tuition fees (Tuition Fee Loan) and one for general living expenses (Maintenance Loan). The amount they'll lend you for maintenance depends on a few things, such as whether you live with your parents and where you study. There's a 'London weighting', which means that anyone fortunate or foolish enough to be studying in the capital will receive more money. Your parents' earnings also play a part in how much you get, with students from lower-income backgrounds eligible for up to 25 per cent extra. The Student Loans Company will want their money back when you finish studying (see 'Paying Back Your Student Loan' later on in this chapter), but this only starts once your annual income exceeds £15,000 and will be deducted automatically from your pay packet.

- **30–50 per cent** is the percentage that living and accommodation costs in London exceed all other regions in the UK.

- **£6,170 + fees** is the maximum a full-time student living away from home can get per academic year studying in London.

- **£5,620 + fees** is the maximum a full-time student living away from home can get per academic year studying anywhere else in the UK.

→ **www.slc.co.uk** – Student Loans Company website, which includes information about the rates of inflation.

→ **www.direct.gov.uk** – Find an online calculator here to give you a rough idea of how much you are eligible to get from a student loan.

Student Overdrafts

Living in the red has more or less become a way of life, which is why most student accounts come with a fat side-order of interest-free overdraft.

Mind you, the banks aren't doing this out of the kindness of their hearts. They're desperate to get you in their pocket as a student, because if you bank with them now, you're likely to continue banking with them for the rest of your life. **Depressingly, you're more likely to get divorced than split with your bank.** The banks will try to reel you in with free kettles, CDs, shower radios, and even the odd credit card. An overdraft is essential for student life, although staying within your overdraft limit can be hard. Provided you can stay within the agreed limit, an interest-free overdraft (effectively an interest-free loan) on your bank account is a great deal, but here are some of the things to check for in the small print:

• The size of the interest-free overdraft they will give you.

• The interest they will charge for going beyond your overdraft. This will usually be between 7 and 10 per cent, if you have agreed it with them beforehand, but could be up to 30 per cent if you haven't. They will also sting you for each letter they send out, because, well, paper is seriously expensive ...

• What their graduate account is like. Many banks let you hold on to your interest-free overdraft for up to three years and will give you preferential rates on graduate loans and mortgages.

• What interest they will pay you, should you ever find yourself in credit.

If you think your bank's been heavyhanded with its fees (charging you for having an overdraft, then charging you again for the letter they sent to tell you you've got an overdraft, that kind of thing) it is possible to challenge them for 'unreasonable charges'. For advice on how to do so – and to see if you have a case to fight – contact the Office of Fair Trading:

→ **www.oft.gov.uk**

Maintenance Grants

A couple of grand, anyone? **About half of the student population is entitled to a maintenance grant towards living costs,** which could mean up to £2,765 a year. More people are eligible for a financial leg-up than think they are, so it's always worth going for income assessment.

Anyone getting the full maintenance grant or paying over a certain amount for tuition fees will get a bursary of 10 per cent or more (generally the range is between £300 and £3,000 a year) from the university itself. Some places are so keen to attract students that they'll give you a bursary regardless – so always ask, whatever your situation.

Particularly bright sparks could apply for a scholarship, though these tend to focus on science and technology, rather than the arts. Most universities also offer a hardship fund for when things go unexpectedly pear-shaped.

→ **www.direct.gov.uk/en/EducationAndLearning/index.htm**
  – Gives lots of information on how much you could
  be entitled to.

> There's additional help for students with dependents, disabilities or specific learning difficulties. In the case of dyslexia, for example, you can get computers, printers, scanners and other electronic wizardry, as long as you have an assessment to prove your condition.
>
> A lot of people have dyslexia and don't even know it; visit the Study Support Team at your university for a free assessment.

Student Jobs

You came to university in search of lifestyle experimentation, new friends and, ultimately, an education. Yet you find yourself dressed in a chicken costume on a damp Saturday night, handing out flyers. The couple of grand a year you get from grants and bursaries doesn't go very far, so extra cash has to come from somewhere. You'll laugh about it one day ...

I was paid a pittance to illustrate the chalkboards in Starbucks!

I made plastic bread for props at the National Theatre.

I stripped naked in front of old men – for Life Drawing at the Working Men's College in Camden for £8 per hour.

I did a week's work experience at *The Times*, and ended up with a job for the next five years.

I did sari modelling in India.

I worked in a sandwich bar: it helped me decide to get into business some day, because the owner was making a fortune!

I did an internship in a shoe design company in Italy. I learnt that I could fit in, but also that I didn't want to. Both valuable lessons.

I had a job in an old people's home. I had to clean fridges, cupboards and surfaces that were already clean and climb inside the ovens to clean them ... horrible.

Tax

You have to pay tax from the day you are born until after you die and students are no exception. If you exceed the annual personal allowance, you're liable to pay tax at the going rate.

If you are being paid for the first time through PAYE (Pay As You Earn), your employer should give you a P46 form that you fill in and send to the Inland Revenue. Until the tax office has processed your form, they will charge you 'Emergency Tax' at the highest possible rate. Don't worry – they'll refund the difference once your status has been assessed. When you leave a job you'll get a P45 to hand on to your next employer.

If you are, or have recently been, self-employed, you will need to fill in an annual self-assesment form to send to the Inland Revenue. You can do this online and the system works out either how much you need to pay or what you are owed.

→ **www.hmrc.gov.uk** – The Inland Revenue website gives details of all personal tax issues.

→ **www.direct.gov.uk/en/MoneyTaxandBenefits/index.htm** – Information on all you need to know about what you're earning and how it'll be taxed.

Paying Back Your Student Loan

Considering the obscene sum you're likely to have borrowed by the time you graduate, paying back your student loan is less painful than you might imagine. To start with, you don't have to hand over a penny until your salary hits £15,000. Then the money to repay the loan comes out of your wages via the PAYE system (along with your tax), before it hits your account, so you don't have to worry about keeping track of bills and remembering to make regular payments. If the digits on your payslip drop below the magic number, you stop paying until it rises over the repayment threshold again. (If you're self-employed, you can either set up a direct debit to the Student Loans Company, or, if you know you have gone over the threshold, put some money aside for when you do your annual tax return.)

Having an outstanding student loan is unlikely to do you much harm, as the interest rates are so low. Of course, if your winning horse comes in, you can pay off the loan early, but, if you do have the money, you may be better off investing it in a high interest savings account. In fact, student loans are such a good deal that some see it as an opportunity to borrow cash cheaply to invest. The longer you remain under the repayment threshold, the more money your investment will make.

However, for all their user-friendly cuddliness, the Student Loans Company is still a lender, not a giver. They will actively pursue you to recover their money, through courts and bailiffs if necessary. If you plan to work out of the country for any length of time, you'll need to make alternative repayment arrangements. Skip town without telling them and they'll start to fine you for defaulting on payments. The Student Loans Company will only write off your loan if you don't manage to hit a £15,000 salary within 25 years, or when you turn 65. Even if you have to declare yourself bankrupt (see the **Ways Out of Debt** chapter), they'll stalk you for monies owed as soon as you start earning again.

The average salary offered in a recent *Prospects Directory* (a graduate recruitment resource) was £22,851 p.a. That's £7,851 over the £15,000 cut-off, so if you're earning this kind of money in your first year of work you'd pay back 9 per cent of that: £706.59 in a year, £58.88 a month or £13.58 a week.

Some average starting salaries by industry:

£22,437 Management consultancy
£20,663 IT
£19,957 Engineering
£18,794 Advertising, marketing and PR
£17,854 HR and employment
£16,032 Publishing, media and performing arts

Postgraduate Study

The last thing you want after leaving university is another few years of belt-tightening – though you'll probably want to keep on with the lifestyle experimentation and make yet more friends – but **recent surveys suggest that holders of postgraduate qualifications tend to earn more** than those with mere degrees. They are also less likely to be unemployed in the first year after graduation. So, while postgraduate study is an expensive option in the short term, the educational benefits may also be matched by financial rewards in the long run.

For all the positives, the bad news about postgraduate study is that the government won't give or lend you a penny (with the exception of those doing teacher training) and there is stiff competition for funding from all other sources.

If your postgraduate study is related to a job, your employer might be persuaded to help with some of the costs. Failing this, there are a number of institutions that give awards (such as the Royal Society or the Arts and Humanities Research Council), as well as government departments and charities with research interests. As with undergraduate degrees, many universities also offer scholarships and some companies offer funding for research they think might be helpful to their own industry.

If you can't find anyone to fund your postgraduate study, then Career Development Loans are deferred loans that you can use to pay up to 80 per cent of course fees. Otherwise, many banks do specific study loans, and if you're doing a PGCE (Postgraduate Certificate of Education) or a DipHE (Diploma of Higher Education) then you can talk to your old friends at the Student Loans Company again.

→ **www.prospects.ac.uk** – UK Official Graduate Careers

→ **www.npc.org.uk** – National Postgraduate Committee

→ **www.rcuk.ac.uk** – Research Council UK

Where to Get Advice

If you really find yourself up cash creek, **there are plenty of paddles floating around.** As a first port of call, most student unions provide general advice and if they can't answer your questions, they'll be able to refer you to other sources of help and information. They may put you in touch with the Citizens Advice Bureau, which offers a range of services, including impartial face-to-face advice on legal and financial matters. If you want anonymity, contact the Student Counselling Helpline or look for the answers to your questions online (see below for a list of websites). Most high street banks have dedicated student liaison staff, who are there to discuss your borrowing needs, problems with repayments or any other issues relating to your account. Remember, though, they are there to make money out of you, so always get independent advice. In the long run, however, negotiating with your bank or building society is likely to be less stressful than the consequences of burying your head in the sand.

→ **www.nusonline.co.uk/info/money** – The financial bit of the NUS website that features a 'funding finder' section. This includes tools for budget planning, searching for funding, loan repayment calculation and future wage predictions.

→ **www.citizensadvice.org.uk** – Citizens Advice Bureau website.

→ **www.direct.gov.uk** – Basic facts and figures in a straightforward format; look at the student finance section.

→ **www.slc.co.uk** – The Student Loans Company website doesn't have as much info, but it's good for phone numbers if you need to call them to sort anything out.

→ **www.moneysavingexpert.com** – UK's most popular independent money site, and has all the vital info you need, along with other gems, like using Lithuanian sim cards to cut your mobile phone bills.

→ **www.creditaction.org.uk** – Credit Action produce a free Student Moneymanual.

Magic Plastic

There's a pub in London with a sign above the bar reading 'Cash is king'. Except that it isn't any more. The king is dead. Back in 2004, the total national spending on cards overtook spending in cash for the first time, and by the following year it was up to over 60 per cent. People flash their plastic for just about anything, from online purchases through to rounds in the pub.

It's not difficult to see why cards are so popular: no more wads of notes stretching your wallet, no more loose change ripping through your pockets and no more having to worry about funny foreign currencies when you go abroad. It's just so easy to spend, spend, spend using plastic – there's none of the pain you'll feel in handing over real money.

cash

As long as you make sure your cards know who's boss, there's nothing to be scared of – some can even save you money.

There's a plethora of cards vying for your purchasing affections, from the common or garden debit card to the much more dangerous credit and store cards. **They can be hazardous creatures if you let them be your master.** Credit cards can make you feel like you aren't really paying for something. Tomorrow, however, comes all too soon, and with it your credit-card statements.

Debit Cards

Anything you spend on a debit card goes out of your account and into the vendor's at the touch of a button. It's pretty much like writing a cheque, but without the waiting around for it to clear. A debit card is a pretty safe way to spend. It will let you go a little into the red, but usually only as far as your overdraft allows. The only caveat is that, as paying with a card is that bit easier than paying with cash, you may well pay more or buy more than you would otherwise.

Credit Cards

A credit card. Your flexible friend, plastic pal or chip-and-pin chum, it allows you to spend money you don't yet have. A credit card differs from a debit card in that, rather than deducting the cost of your purchases from the money in your account, it puts it on a bill which you settle up later, effectively letting you delay payment. In essence, it's an immediate, pre-approved loan – albeit an expensive one. Therein lies the rub. If you don't settle the bill on time, you have to pay interest on the money you are borrowing, and those rates tend to be very high. Plus if you don't keep up with the minimum payments, you get to pay fines on top of that.

Getting cash from an ATM is expensive
Most cards will slap interest on the cash from the moment it comes out of the machine. What's more, interest rates for cash are usually much higher than for purchases. This also applies for transactions in foreign bureaux de changes and sometimes even for purchases of gift vouchers.

How credit cards work
Most credit-card companies will send you a monthly bill, detailing the total amount you owe them, the minimum payment you need to make that month, and the date the money needs to reach them by. This date can be a tad misleading, since cheques and even bank transfers all take time to clear, so for the funds to hit your account by that specific day, you actually have to pay several days earlier. There are fines for paying late, which used

to be quite hefty – standard charges tended to be £20 to £25 – but since 2006 have been capped at a much more palatable £12. (God bless the Office of Fair Trading.)

The minimum payment is usually between 2 and 5 per cent of the total balance, but it's worth paying back more if you can possibly afford it. There are a few different ways that the credit-card companies charge interest (see below). Most of these ways are compound – which simply means that the interest is not kept separate but added to the total balance for the next month, so you are effectively paying interest on interest. The smaller your balance, the less interest there will be and the more chance you have of getting on top of it sooner. It may cost you a couple more quid now but it'll save you a whole heap of notes in the future.

> **Fixed interest** is when the lender agrees to charge the same rate of interest for a fixed period, regardless of what the market is doing.

> **Variable interest** is when the interest rate fluctuates, usually depending on external influences. If you see the term 'tracker' it means that these variations are directly related to the Bank of England base rate.

> **Capped interest** is when the interest moves with official rates, but cannot rise above a pre-arranged level. If the rate is termed 'collared' then there will also be a minimum level that it cannot fall below.

Choosing a credit card

Comparing credit cards is a tricky business. The plastic market-place is a busy and competitive one, and everyone is keen to get you (and your debt) on board. They will do this with a heady mix of introductory deals, crafty marketing and competing offers, and the most important rule is that loyalty counts for naught. Always keep your beady eyes open, and if you find a better card than the one you currently have, then change it.

When we went shopping for a credit card we found rates varying between 6.8 and 19.9 per cent and if you add in store cards you'll find rates of 25 per cent and beyond.

One way to compare credit cards is by their APR. This Annual Percentage Rate takes into account the interest rate plus all the other hidden and administrative charges to give you a suppos-edly realistic picture of exactly how much a card will cost you each year. Unfortunately such figures can be massaged to give a rosier picture than reality – for example a recent study by the consumer watchdog Which? alleged that among the UK's top 20 card companies there were 12 different methods being used to calculate APRs – but combined with careful reading of the small print an APR can still be a useful point of comparison.

If you already have an outstanding balance on credit cards, one of the easiest ways to save yourself money is by a balance transfer. Many credit-card companies will try and tempt you by offering you an introductory APR of 0 per cent on debts from another card that you transfer over to them. Though these offers usually only last for six months to a year, the fact that your debt isn't growing means that you can pay it off double quick. Also, there's not generally anything to stop you swapping financial partners after this interest-free honeymoon period is over. Of course there are things that can sour an otherwise sweet deal, so roll up your sleeves and delve into the small print. You're looking for things like transfer fees and any clauses that

allow the credit-card company to backpedal. Some will reserve the right to cancel your interest-free period if you go over your limit or are late paying.

Warning signs to look out for include any fees payable just for having the card (these used to be pretty rare, but are coming back as competition drives APRs down).

> Credit-card debt is expensive. There are almost always cheaper ways to borrow money; use those to pay off your credit cards (see the **Moving Money** chapter).

Credit cards and fraud

Credit-card fraud is one of the tabloids' favourite scare stories – and there are a lot of scams out there, from cards being cloned and used on the other side of the world to full-on identity theft.

The good news is that credit-card companies keep an increasingly close eye on your account. It's not unusual to get a call from your bank seconds after you make a big purchase just to make sure it is you using the card. It's also good to know that if you are the victim of card fraud you'll usually get your money back. In practice, cards are safer than cash. Lose cash and you'll never get it back, lose your card and you'll almost certainly be covered.

Many people don't read through their credit-card statements – finding it too painful – which means that dodgy transactions can sneak through unnoticed. It may come as a surprise to discover that while you were at work in Leeds, you were also getting cash out of an ATM in Madrid ...

Tips for the thrifty

Play a smart game and you can make money out of your credit card. Most card companies offer perks – which they hope will tempt you into choosing their card and then never use. (It's how gyms make their money!) These include:

• Free travel insurance. If you buy your holiday using your card, you may get free travel insurance

• Online protection. Some cards will offer you protection against fraudulent use

• Purchase protection. Cards often offer cover against accidental damage and theft on anything you buy using the card

• Delivery protection. Some cards cover purchases made online or over the phone, reimbursing you if they don't arrive or get damaged during the delivery

• Points can mean prizes – airmiles, discounts and free gifts can all save you cash, but only if you were in the market for the item already ...

→ **www.moneynet.co.uk** – A good source for helping you choose a card and a useful link for comparing credit cards.

→ **www.about-credit-cards.co.uk**–Another helpful comparison site.

→ **www.fool.co.uk** – Helps compare all types of financial products, including credit cards.

→ **www.moneysupermarket.com** – A very useful place to find out what different cards have to offer you.

Loyalty Cards

Of the various species of plastic making their home in your wallet, the loyalty card is among the most benign, because you don't use it to pay for things. You get it free of charge from participating stores.

What do you get?

Normally the way it works is that when you buy something, the card records what you bought and the amount you spent and translates it into points. The more you spend, the more points you get, and occasionally special promotions let you double or even triple your points on selected items. For some reason this usually seems to be on completely arbitrary items like cat food or washing up liquid. Amass enough points and you can trade them in for rewards that range from discounts to free gifts. Shops also sometimes give VIP treatment to people with loyalty cards. A clothes store for example might flirt with your affections by giving you access to a new celebrity-designed collection the night before everyone else, coupled with free alcohol to loosen your purse strings.

And what does the store get?

Funnily enough, although your loyalty to their brand is a happy bonus, it's not the stores' prime motivation. These schemes cost a fortune to operate, and what the companies are really after is information. What you buy is recorded so analysts can monitor your spending habits. They can see what sells, what doesn't, and how different sectors of society are splashing their cash.

Loyalty schemes

There are loyalty card schemes that aren't tied to just one shop – just like the way some credit cards give you points wherever you use the card. This works nicely for all concerned. You get rewards for your various shoppings, while the companies involved get to see how you unload your hard-earned cash across a variety of markets. Not only this, but they also get to share the costs of running the scheme.

The most widespread – and widely known – loyalty-card schemes in the UK include the Nectar Card, Tesco Clubcard and Boots Advantage Card. Nectar is the most all-encompassing; it began in Sainsbury's but now has a number of companies affiliated to it. These include Debenhams, BP, Hertz, Dollond & Aitchison, and even Gala Bingo – meaning you can earn points for buying new clothes to wear for your appointment to have your eyesight corrected before you put petrol in your hire car so you can drive to bingo, after popping into the supermarket to do your weekly shop. No matter how mundane all those things may seem to you, every time you do any one of them, those data analysts get very excited.

Store Cards

If a credit card and a loyalty card got carried away one balmy evening after a plate of oysters and a bottle of Chilean red, the resulting offspring would be a store card. It's a credit card that you can only use in certain shops.

What do you get?

There has to be a reason for you to start using a store card in the first place, so shops will usually offer you some kind of cheerful introductory discount on your day's purchases in exchange for taking one out. You fill in the form at the counter and, subject to a quick credit check, you can walk away with a store card there and then. You then use it to pay for your shopping, and at the end of the month, as with a credit card, you get a bill through the post. As well as giving you this initial sweetener, store cards may carry continuing discounts each time you use them. They sometimes also offer many of the benefits of loyalty cards, such as spend-and-save points and exclusive cardholder offers.

What does the store get?

The downside to store cards is their extraordinarily high APRs. As a rule, they're much more expensive than credit cards, with some charging nearly 30 per cent interest, making them one of the most expensive ways to borrow money. Around two thirds of the store cards in Britain charge more than 25 per cent. That's not to say that they should be avoided altogether. It's perfectly reasonable to take one out, rinse the introductory discount, pay the bill off as soon as it arrives then put the card at the bottom of your sock drawer until they offer you some-thing else worth using it for. Or if you really don't trust yourself then you could get to work on it with the kitchen scissors.

As with all forms of card, it's all about exploiting the plastic potential to your own benefit.

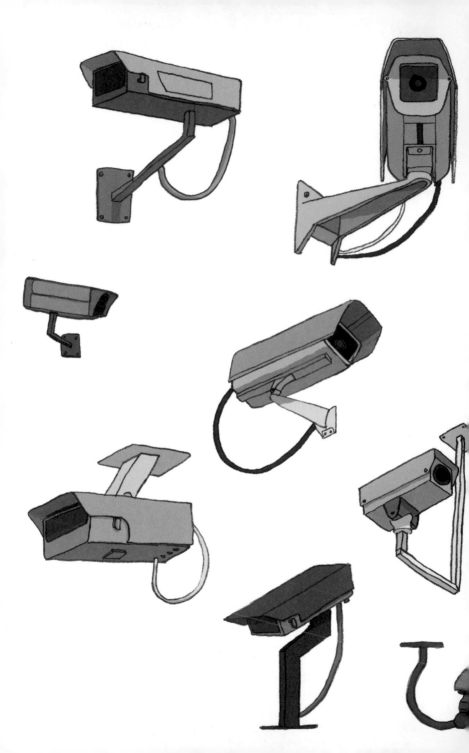

Credit Rating

Big Brother is most definitely watching. Short of living under an assumed name, working cash in hand and keeping your savings in gold bullion, **it's difficult to avoid leaving little electronic footprints wherever you go**, and this is particularly true with regards to your credit history.

Records of your financial past are kept by credit reference agencies (CRAs), and when you apply for credit of any kind, whether it's a mortgage, a credit card, a loan or a buy-now-pay-later deal on a sportscar, the company putting up the cash will check out your history with a CRA.

CRAs can give a 'credit rating' of how good a debtor you are, but more often they simply provide a collection of facts about you which the lender then uses to make their own judgement about whether you are their sort of person.

The more alarming the facts, or the worse your rating, the less you'll be able to borrow, and the higher the interest rate will be for you.

Credit Reference Agencies (CRAs)

The three main CRAs are Experian, Equifax and Callcredit, and they share information. There are lots of things that will appear on your credit report, some of which may damage your chances of getting further credit. Some of these gremlins in the machinery might be:

Late payments on loans – this includes the credit-card statement accidentally left on the kitchen table until after the due date. Lenders want to know if you are unreliable.

Bankruptcies and county court judgements (CCJs) – if you have a history of letting down your creditors in a serious way, this will count against you when trying to borrow more.

Multiple credit checks in a short period of time – though companies are not allowed to see whether other people have turned you down for credit, all of the checks carried out over the last 12 months are visible on your file. If there are an abnormal number, it may mean that you've had a lot of applications declined or that you've been trying to borrow a lot of money, both of which set alarm bells ringing.

Not being on the electoral roll – you being properly registered provides a degree of protection for the lender. They may be suspicious if you aren't.

A number of other things can influence your score, such as being a homeowner (or not), being self-employed (or in employment at all), and being financially tied up with someone who has a ropey credit history. It's worth knowing, however, that joint accounts are the only occasion when lenders are able to link your rating to that of your other half. So, keep separate bank accounts if you don't want a grim bank balance to get in the way of true love.

Who's Checking on You?

A lot of people, apparently. Apart from the obvious ones – such as credit-card companies, banks and building societies – people who want to find out about you include anyone selling you something on credit or in instalments, such as gas, electricity, and mobile phones. Only authorized companies can access your credit rating. If, for example, an employer wanted to know your credit rating (and some do), they would have to ask you to get a report and send it to them.

It isn't the CRA that approves or turns you down for credit, they only supply the figures. It's the person who's asked for the check who decides

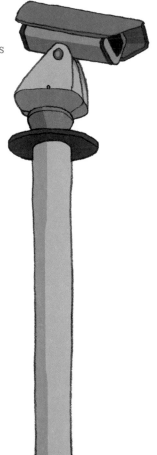

The addresses of the three main credit reference agencies

Experian
→ www.experian.co.uk
  Consumer Help Service
  Experian Ltd
  PO Box 8000
  Nottingham NG80 7WF

Equifax
→ www.equifax.co.uk
  Equifax Plc
  Credit File Advice Centre
  PO Box 1140
  Bradford BD1 5US

Callcredit
→ www.callcredit.co.uk
  Consumer Services Team
  Callcredit Plc
  PO Box 491
  Leeds LS3 1WZ

Finding Out About Your Credit Rating

You too can access your credit rating. If you've been refused credit, find out which CRA the lender used (however painful it may be to talk to them). Write to the CRA, enclosing your name, address, the name of your business (if you have one) and any other places you've lived over the previous six years.

Some companies sell expensive credit monitoring and 'repair' services, but access to the basic facts of the report is a statutory right, and will set you back a princely £2, so do it yourself.

When you get hold of the results, check them for mistakes, which do occur every now and again. If there are a lot of mistakes, it may be that some sly soul has been trying to use your identity for their own purposes. If there's this kind of good explanation for a rocky patch in your past, then you'll be able to get an explanatory note attached to your file. Also be sure to check the basic personal details, such as your address, are correct.

Improving Your Credit Rating

If all responsibility lies squarely on your own shoulders, then never fear. There are a number of ways you can improve your credit rating:

Get on the electoral roll – if you aren't already, then get on it (whether or not you intend to vote). Then tell the CRA straight away.

Distance yourself from other people's debt – it's best not to have a joint bank account with someone who has a bad credit rating, as it will be linked to yours. If your name has already become embroiled with someone else's, you can go to the website of one of the big CRAs where you can download a Notice of Disassociation.

Cancel any unused credit cards – an enormous amount of available credit, even if you're not using it all, looks bad. Just keep the ones you use.

Start using credit cards – sounds odd this one, but there are folk who get refused credit simply because they've never had any before – having no rating at all can make companies suspicious. Some people don't like the idea of having a credit card, but provided you pay off the bills when they come, and you're not paying fees just for having the card, it's nothing to be afraid of.

Spend and pay up – this might take a little time, but it's the only way to fix a damaged credit rating. Take out a couple of credit cards and use them as much as you can within your budget (for things like petrol and grocery shopping), while making absolutely sure that when the bills arrive, you pay them immediately. All of this positive traffic on your cards will send out the message that you're a trustworthy soul and, given time, that information should make its way on to your credit rating.

> If you have been made bankrupt, have a CCJ or have defaulted on a loan the blot will stay on your copybook for 6 years – in the case of defaults on loans that's counting from when you settle the debt, not from when you took the loan out. Nonetheless, the more you do to appear to be a good risk, the better.
>
> If it's just a case of a few missed payments on a credit card, a few months of good behaviour should sort it out.

Moving Money

There are all kinds of reasons why you might find yourself moving money between accounts. You might open up an account so you can put money aside for monthly debt repayments, you might want to squirrel some money away into a higher interest bond or you might just like filling out forms. Just as you can transfer a positive balance, you can sometimes move negative ones, and now and then there are very good reasons for doing this.

Moving your debts between accounts can save you money, for example, by transferring an outstanding credit-card balance to an account with 0 per cent APR introductory offers, or by consolidating your debt. What debt consolidation means is taking out one big loan to pay off all your other debts. Putting all your eggs in one basket, so to speak. This means that the loan is bigger, but you usually have longer to pay it off, and often the repayments per month are smaller.

Types of Money Movement

Credit cards

One good way of managing credit-card debt is to keep your debt moving between cards. It might sound peculiar, but by shuffling your credit-card debts around, you can often save yourself money. This is because there are plenty of credit cards offering special introductory offers of 0 per cent APR on balance transfers from other credit cards, usually for the first six months or so. After that they'll probably come down on you hard, but by then you may well have spirited your lack of money on to someone else offering the same deal. A sort of Scarlet Pimpernel of debtors.

There are things to watch out for with this strategy, of course. First amongst these are transfer fees. Some companies might not tap you for interest straight off, but instead will drop a hefty one-off transfer charge on you. You'll need to look out for this in the small print before you sign on the dotted line. As long as there are no sly charges on the card you've chosen and you keep track of when you need to move your balance on then it makes good financial sense to be a card tart.

→ **www.confused.com** – Advice and information on which credit cards are offering good introductory offers.

Secured and unsecured loans

If there seem to be a number of debts floating around with your name on them, it can be a good thing to lump them all together in one convenient bundle and get one big loan to pay off all the smaller ones. Rates on loans are generally much better than on credit cards, and the better the interest rates are, the sooner you can pay off your debts. There are two kinds of loans: secured and unsecured. A secured loan is where you agree to sell something significant – such as your house – if you can't pay up; these will get you the cheapest interest rates.

Unsecured loans are when someone lends you money and then has to trust that you will pay them back, as there's nothing valuable 'securing' the loan if you don't pay. As a result, interest rates on unsecured loans are usually a lot higher than for secured loans.

→ **www.moneysupermarket.com/loans** – Rate comparisons for various types of loan.

Benefits of consolidation
There are benefits to consolidation loans, but you've got to keep your eyes open and play your cards right.

First of all, there's the rates. If your debts are mostly on credit cards, then even an unsecured loan with a bank is liable to offer a lower rate of interest. The way to get the best rates, of course, is by taking out a secured loan, if you have something to secure it with. The reason for this is that lenders will view you as more of a sure thing if you've got more to lose by not paying up, and the creditor is pretty sure they'll get their money back (for example by making you sell your house if that's what you've used to secure the loan) and this decreased risk for them translates into lower costs for you.

Lower interest rates generally mean lower monthly instalments, and if you can afford to keep paying the same amount as you have been previously, then those overpayments will start to soak up your debts in double quick time. From an administrative point of view, a consolidation loan is also a breath of fresh air, as rather than juggling a variety of creditors all wanting different amounts of money at different times, you now have just one monthly payment to one company. In simple terms of stress and time, you're onto a winner.

Disadvantages of consolidation

That's not to say that taking out a consolidation loan doesn't have its pitfalls. The trick to sussing them out is to focus on what you can't see straight away – like a magic eye puzzle, but without going cross-eyed and getting a headache. There can be lots of one-off fees involved both in taking out the new loan and in winding up the old ones which can make things a little harder just to start with, and many companies will try and heap hidden charges on top of what you think you're paying.

If you've got the time to watch daytime TV you'll have seen those ads that loan shark companies put on. There's a reason they're known as loan sharks and not loan puppies; they're not cute, loyal or cuddly. If they give you a hefty payout, then there will not be 'money left over for a holiday' or 'a bit to put by for the kids'. Their interest rates are often frighteningly high. Have a look at that very small print that flashes across the screen for the minimum legal number of seconds just before the end of the advert. It will tell you the estimated growth of an average loan when paid back over a standard number of years, and it does not make happy reading. Their object is to trick you into borrowing as much money as possible then milk you as their cash cow for the rest of your natural days.

One particularly sneaky dog to look out for is something called PPI. This stands for Payment Protection Insurance, and is often popped on top of your bills without you realizing it. PPI means that if for some reason (redundancy or prolonged illness being common ones) you can't keep up with your payments, then they should be covered by the company for an agreed period (see opposite for more).

Paying something back over a long period of time has its downsides. Though it might offer you a little relief in the short term, making smaller payments over a larger number of years can mean that even at a lower rate you end up paying back far more than you previously owed. The faster you can pay off your loan, the slower it will grow and the less you will eventually repay.

If you've gone for a secured loan then you've got the best rates, but you've also raised the stakes. Since it's usually your home you put up as collateral, the consequences of not keeping up your payments are more extreme. It's a big step. Having said that, you're using your capital to maximize your potential to paying off your debts, not throwing your house keys onto the table in a game of poker. There's nothing to fear if you've thought everything through carefully.

Payment Protection Insurance might seem like a good idea in principle, but ideally whatever money you're handing over to insure your payments could be better used actually paying off the debts. Also, for a lot of people, PPI is not strictly necessary and may not even pay out – you probably won't be covered for periods of unemployment if you work on short contracts for example.

If you have any savings they could be used as a safety buffer to cover missed payments, and quite a lot of people have some kind of professional insurance that will cover them anyway, leaving them effectively paying twice for cover that they can only claim on once.

The jury's still out on PPI. It might be that in your case it's a good idea, but it's always worth making sure in which situations you're covered, and how much you're paying for it. If you decide to take out PPI, then shop around for policies, and look out for any loopholes that will mean the policy doesn't have to pay you. Check, for instance, if there are any special situations for the self-employed, and whether any income support you might happen to receive will be affected by the insurance payouts.

→ **www.moneysavingexpert.com/insurance/cheap-loan-insurance** – Martin Lewis, the Money Saving Expert's thoughts about PPI.

What to do before you take out a consolidation loan

First of all, run through your numbers. This needn't be too difficult, but if it's all too painful to look at, then get someone to run through them for you. Get hold of the APR (Annual Percentage Rate) for the loan. This is the total cost of borrowing from someone, including interest, one-off payments and hidden administration charges. It's a legal requirement that companies provide you with this information, and it should give you a decent idea of how much you will eventually end up paying back.

Next, have a good sift through all the terms and conditions. Check how the interest rate will change through the lifetime of the loan, and look for the consequences of not paying, or of paying late. Some loans may give good rates but catch you out by stinging you for stumping up after the due date. Keep a beady eye out for companies charging PPI or extra fees for 'debt management plans'. Some of these are very pricey, but are piggybacked on top of your monthly payments so you might not necessarily notice.

If the numbers don't add up, then don't take out a secured loan to consolidate your debts, as there is a lot at stake. They tend to be long-term plans, and as such are not the best option for everyone. For many people it may be quicker and cheaper to pay off their debts in another way.

Alternatives to consolidating debts

Getting a consolidation loan is a big thing, particularly if you're putting up your house as collateral, and you need to know that you're not going to end up paying back enough to fund a small country.

A big alternative to getting a consolidation loan is to look at remortgaging. If you happen to be ensconced in your dream home and paying your mortgage each month, then the sums you are dealing with are huge. Even if you've started with an attractive introductory offer, you usually tend to slip on to your mortgage provider's standard rate after a while, so it's definitely worth shopping around for lower interest mortgages. At this sort of level the tiniest variation in a portion of a percentage can mean an enormous saving, so switching from a standard variable rate mortgage to a lower rate one can free up a whole pile of cash for sorting out your other debts.

For suggestions tailored to your particular circumstances, have a look at the website for the Consumer Credit Counselling Service. There's an easy CCCS Debt Remedy questionnaire that you can fill in (anonymously if you wish) and in 20 minutes or so they'll shoot you over a personalized plan of action. This ought to let you know whether getting a consolidation loan is right for you, or whether there are other things you might try first.

→ **www.cccs.co.uk** – Consumer Credit Counselling Service for advice on consolidating loans.

→ **www.moneysavingexpert.com** – Martin Lewis has a large section on consolidated loans which you may want to reference.

Ways Out of Debt

Even if you went into debt with your eyes wide open and with everything looking great on the big balance sheet, things can go wrong. Interest rates change, housing markets crash, **money you counted on getting never arrives – some relatives live for ever.**

If your debt has turned into a bit of a runaway train, then you may have to look at more dramatic solutions than simple careful spending and proactive saving. There are quite a few such measures, including debt management plans, individual voluntary agreements (IVAs) and bankruptcy, and the good news is that there are also a lot of doors you can knock at for help and advice.

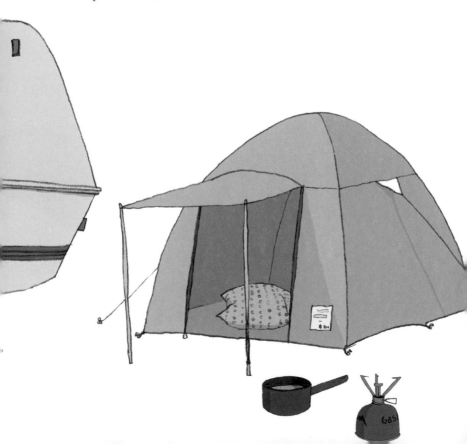

Help and Advice

You never need walk this road alone. Bankruptcy and IVAs are complicated procedures, but **fortunately there are lots of organizations that will give you free, independent advice and hold your hand** as you navigate your way through hard times. The 'free' and 'independent' bits are important. There are lots of companies out there with helpful and official sounding names who are neither, so it's a good idea to team up with one of the friendly organizations listed below.

National Insolvency Service

Just about all the information you could want about any aspect of insolvency is on the National Insolvency Service website and, for a government body, it is mercifully easy to find your way around. Most of it takes the form of bite-size leaflets that you can view online or download as PDFs to print out.

→ **www.insolvency.gov.uk**

The Citizens' Advice Bureau (CAB)

The people in this community charity (it's free) frequently deal with insolvencies, and if nothing else they will be able to point you at trustworthy specialists such as solicitors and accountants. There's lots of information on their website, including how to find your nearest CAB office.

→ **www.citizensadvice.org.uk**

The Consumer Credit Counselling Service

Again, this one's a charity, so the advice is free. The CCCS are also able to arrange and manage Debt Management Plans (DMPs). As well as hosting lots of advice about solutions to debt problems, their website has information about bankruptcy and IVAs. They also have a freephone helpline, online debt counselling and email service.

→ **www.cccs.co.uk** (type this in carefully as there's also a private company at c-c-c-s.com)
Phone 0800 138 1111

→ National Debtline

The other major national debt counselling charity, National Debtline offer many of the same services as the CCCS, including lots of well presented facts, figures and solutions.

www.nationaldebtline.co.uk (type this in carefully as there's also a private company at nationaldebitline.co.uk)

Phone 0808 808 4000

> Watch out: there's always someone with their eye out for a quick buck, and internet search engines don't make a distinction between the good and bad companies. Sometimes it can be difficult to tell which are the charities and which are private companies looking to turn a profit from your debts.

Plan of Action

Bankruptcy isn't the only way out and should be seen as a last resort, rather than a quick solution. Assuming you've done all the budgeting you can, sold off your country home and let the butler go (see **Budgeting** chapter), there are alternative solutions to debts you can't pay.

Informal agreements

If they realize things are really that bad, many lenders will settle for whatever they can get. It's possible to come to an agreement with the individual companies you owe money to. After negotiation, you can make an offer and seek a voluntary agreement. As ever, it's worth getting someone from one of the above organizations to help you.

The secret here is to do things in the right order. Make a list of priority and non-priority debts. Priority debts are ones where if you don't pay you lose something really important (like your place to live, or your electricity and water), and these are the ones you should try and sort out first.

Debt management plans

These can be arranged by one of the charitable services listed earlier in the chapter and are often a great solution as they allow people to clear the entire debt but without the need to pay for the service, borrow more, and with minimal impact on their credit rating. The ongoing support offered by the charitable service in sticking to the plan is also valuable.

Many people avoid the unpleasant side effects of going bankrupt by simply writing directly to their creditors one by one and proposing solutions and compromises. This is an informal way of doing things, but if done carefully it can work. The key to doing so is making sure that you get good advice when making agreements and never agreeing to something you can't afford, just to get someone off your back. Generally, your creditors know they will be better off without the courts being involved and, as long as you are realistic about what you are agreeing to, you'll be better off too.

→ **www.creditaction.org.uk/advice/selfhelp.htm** – Credit Action produces a free 'Dealing with Debt' guide available for download here.

Individual Voluntary Agreements (IVA)

The next step up is an Individual Voluntary Agreement, or IVA. This is much the same as contacting creditors individually, except that it is done through a court in one fell swoop. You make one big proposal to your creditors, and if they accept it, then the agreement becomes legally binding.

You start the process by hiring an insolvency practitioner, who applies to the court for what is called an 'interim order'. This stops anyone hounding you while you're working out the IVA. You decide what you'll offer, and the insolvency practitioner calls a meeting for all your creditors where he puts your proposal to them. If 75 per cent or more of the creditors (in debt value, not number of people) agree to what you suggest, then the rest have to go with it. An IVA stays on your file for six years like a bankruptcy, but is free of the other unwelcome trappings.

Administration orders

There's also another legal procedure called an administration order. If you have debts of less than £ 5,000 but one or more of your creditors takes you to court over it, you can be ordered to make regular payments (usually weekly or monthly) to the court towards clearing your debts. It's important to keep up the payments, or they might end up bankrupting you.

Court proceedings

If your debts get to the stage where your creditors are demanding their money, usually the first thing that will happen is that your case will be taken to a local Magistrates' Court. If, however, your creditors aren't able to get their money back that way (i.e. if you don't have the money to pay them), they will probably apply for what is called 'a judgement' in the County Court. The court will send you a 'claim', which tells you how much is being claimed by your creditors and how much you will also owe in court costs. At the same time they should send you something called a response pack with three forms, two of which you will need to return if you are contesting the claim. One of the forms is for you to return if you want more time to be able to pay.

If you don't do anything, the matter will be dealt with without your input, which means the court will decide on the action to be taken against you. You will be ordered to pay and if you still can't (or won't) pay, the County Court may pass your details on to the government's insolvency office, part of HM Customs and Revenue, which may lead to you being declared bankrupt. You will probably not even be required to attend the courts, all these actions can take place without you being there. If HM Customs and Revenue believes that you could afford to pay the debts and yet you haven't, you could end up in prison.

Debt-collecting agencies and bailiffs

Hopefully you will never get to the stage when the bogeymen come knocking, but should the worst happen there are a couple of things you should know.

There are various types of bailiffs, including county court bailiffs, certificated bailiffs and private bailiffs. Their powers vary, but all of them need an official document called a warrant, and should also give you warning of their visit. Any police present are not there to help the bailiffs, but merely to prevent a breach of the peace.

Bailiffs can only gain what is called peaceful entry, meaning that they can hop over walls and enter through open doors and windows but they can't break anything. If everything is locked down tight then they will leave, but they will be back, so you need to get in touch with whoever you owe money to and find some other kind of solution (see page 60). Once inside your home, bailiffs will try and find property of value (though they can't take anything you need for your work or living essentials) and will arrange for it to be sold at auction.

Bankruptcy

Bankruptcy isn't a 'get out of jail free' card, it's a serious thing with serious repercussions. However, if your back is really against the wall and you've explored all the alternatives, it can be a sound financial move. What's more, in a society where debt is the rule rather than the exception, other people are starting to see it that way too.

What is bankruptcy?

When you need to pay back more than you've got, you are in trouble. Sooner or later creditors will start demanding their money. If they get really tired of waiting they may declare you bankrupt, which means a court will force you to pay them as much as you can.

There's a popular myth that bankruptcy involves making all your debts disappear and you can just wipe the slate clean and start over again. In reality, life as a bankrupt is a lot tougher than that. Bankruptcy is a legal status that means you've thrown in your cards and handed over your affairs to an 'official receiver' who sells off all your non-essential assets (property, possessions, savings) to pay back as much as you can of your debts. You also have to abide by a number of pretty strict rules about how you manage your finances while bankrupt. The state of bankruptcy usually lasts for a year (although it can be less), but the effects can last much longer. After that year most of your debts are cancelled.

Should I go bankrupt?
There's no easy answer to this one. If you do decide to declare bankruptcy, you will lose your debts, but you'll probably lose most of what you own as well - it's an extremely tough decision to make.

There are other escape routes, including tighter regulation of your outgoings and intermediate steps like debt consolidation (see the **Moving Money** chapter). If something more drastic is needed to breathe life into your ailing finances then there are different courses of action, not as extreme as bankruptcy, that let you arrange things directly with your creditors. You can find out more about these at the end of this chapter.

Bankruptcy is an increasingly personal thing – it is something that can happen to anyone, not just someone running a business. Here are some UK-wide figures from the second quarter of 2007:

3,032 – The number of company liquidations

16,258 – The number of individual bankruptcies

10,698 – The number of people who took Individual Voluntary Agreements, also known as IVAs

26,956 – The total number of individuals who declared themselves insolvent (i.e. either going bankrupt or taking an IVA)

4.2 per cent – The increase of individuals who declared themselves insolvent, compared to the second quarter of 2006

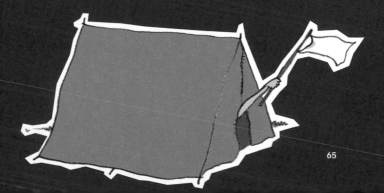

What happens next?

You may be in a situation where you have no choice. You may have got to the glum position where bankruptcy is the only thing that makes sense, or you may find yourself declared bankrupt by someone else, whether you like it or not.

The procedure varies depending on the individual case, but it will kick off by either you or a creditor, to whom you owe more than £750 in unsecured loans, sending off a form to the London High Court or your local county court. This is called a bankruptcy petition, and as a result of this the court may issue a bankruptcy order. Whether or not you have filed the petition yourself, you must co-operate as fully as possible when the order arrives.

Next, the court appoints an official receiver who will interview you and make a list of your liabilities (your debts) and your assets (the things you own). They will then decide whether to act as your trustee themselves or to appoint an insolvency practitioner as the trustee.

The trustee's job is to use your assets to pay off as much debt as possible. This may mean selling your home, if you own it, along with any other valuables. It will almost certainly mean closing any business you own and dismissing your employees. Redundant employees and the administrative costs of the bankruptcy are among the first claims to be paid out, followed by the rest of your creditors. Sometimes there's money left over in the end, in which case you'll get that back. If there's a shortfall the trustee may give you an income payment order, which means you agree to hand over a portion of your income for a set amount of time. These payments can continue for up to three years, but the trustee will always make sure they leave you enough for your general living expenses. If you take a pay cut during the time, then let the court know and they'll adjust your payments accordingly.

What you have to carry on paying

One of the most pleasing things about the whole procedure is that very few of your creditors can come knocking on your door demanding money. Being bankrupt means they have to deal with the trustee, not you. There are, of course, exceptions:

Secured debts – These are where you have promised to give something of value to the creditor if you don't pay your debt. So, in the case of a mortgage, either you keep up repayments or the lender can take the house.

Child maintenance payments and fines ordered by a court – You have to keep on paying these.

Benefit overpayments – If you've had more than your fair share in benefits then the government will sort out any discrepancy by deducting it from future payments.

Student loans – Yes, sad this one. Because these are paid back in a different way from other loans, you still have to keep on repaying at whatever rate is appropriate to your salary (see the **Student Life** chapter).

What you can hold onto

When you go bankrupt, you hand over all of your assets to a trustee to sell off. Fortunately though, they can't quite take the shirt off your back. These are the things you don't have to hand over:

Stuff you need for work – this could be anything from your tools to a Transit van, provided it's used by you personally.

The essentials – such as clothes, furniture, general household items and anything else that you need to live your life in relative comfort. Unfortunately you'll find it hard to prove that your iPhone and Xbox are essentials.

The consequences

These days, it's easier to bounce back from a bankruptcy than ever before, but there are also special rules called 'bankruptcy restrictions orders' (see opposite) that will apply to you. The general term for these is 12 months, though the court can decide to reduce this. They can also increase it to up to 15 years if they think you've been particularly naughty.

Regardless of how long you remain in a state of bankruptcy, the whole business will stay on your file for six years, during which time all kinds of people will be able to check it. These could include prospective landlords and employers, as well as anyone you're asking for more credit – you may not get refused, but you can bet that you'll have to pay a higher interest rate as a high-risk customer.

When the six years is up, if everything has gone to plan, you will be free of the trappings of your bankruptcy and your debts. Even after those six years, though, bankruptcy will still affect your life. With some loans, for example, lenders will ask whether you have ever been bankrupt and you are legally obliged to tell them the truth.

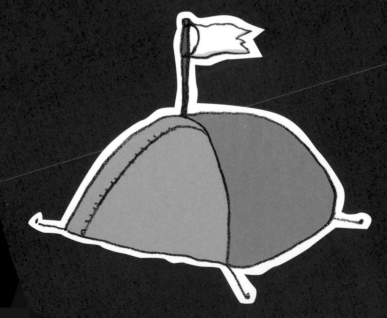

Bankruptcy restrictions orders

There are things that are criminal offences for a bankrupt, and trying any of them could get you into a whole lot of hot water. It is illegal for a bankrupt to:

• Get more than £500 of fresh credit without owning up to your bankruptcy; this includes applying for a new credit card. (You can still apply for, and may get, credit – but you need to be honest about your bankruptcy, and you will pay the cost in higher interest rates.)

• Do business under a different name from the one you went bankrupt under.

• Be concerned (directly or indirectly) in the management of a limited company or be a director without the permission of the court.

• Hold certain public offices, or be a trustee of a charity or pension fund.

Budgeting

Budgeting is all about balancing the cash you have coming in and the cash you have going out. You may have to overcome a natural reluctance to look at bills and statements but once you do, and you start keeping track of them, you'll be much, much better off – financially and emotionally. Treats will no longer be tainted with the bitterness of guilt, but will become pleasures enjoyed because you know that you can afford them.

How to Make a Budget

Look at budgeting both in the short term (start holding on to receipts) and long – one-off extravagances such as holidays and new cars need to be accommodated alongside the regular, monthly cycles of rent, food bills and wages.

Making a budget will take you a little time – at least one cup of tea and several biscuits. Begin by hunting out all your last year's bills, payslips and bank statements (remembering to take account of anything you've popped on the credit card).

Next the outgoings. These are trickier so guestimate if need be. Start with the regular sums, like rent (or mortgage payments), loan repayments, utility bills (including internet), taxes, insurance of various sorts and your mobile phone. Don't forget all the direct debits you've set up and forgotten over the years. Ask your bank for a list. If you have online banking you'll be able to see details of them there.

Next work out the more ad-hoc essentials, such as transport and food (remember the cat, if you have one). Add to this payments covering credit-card bills. You now have the bare essentials.

Oscar Wilde said 'give me the luxuries and I can dispense with the necessities'. Have a stab at working out how much you spend on life's little pleasures. Takeaways, nights on the lash, clothes, CDs, films about gun-toting, musclebound superheroes and everything else that makes existence worthwhile.

Finally, jot down the big expenses, like any holidays you've taken and the yearly financial haemorrhage of the festive season. You now have everything that's coming in on one side (wages), and everything that's going out on the other (everything else).

Have a biscuit (or something stronger) if need be, then set about working out how you're going to make the two sides balance. It might be that it's the luxuries that have to take a hit,or you may decide to apply yourself to finding cheaper deals on your utilities or mortgage, or making the savings by buying supermarkets' own budget-brand food instead of more expensive special stuff. It'll all depend on your personal priorities, but at least you'll know what sort of numbers you're playing with.

Once your budget has got your finances under control, there may come a day when you've got money left over at the end of each month, even after you have drenched yourself in luxury. That's when you can get to grips with some real financial fun – putting your money to work.

→ **www.moneymadeclear.fsa.gov.uk/tools/budget_calculator. html** – A great budget calculator.

Painless Ways to Manage Your Money

Once you have your budget all sorted out, you know how much you spend on daily, monthly, and yearly expenses, and **you are frighteningly aware of precisely how much bacon you're bringing home each month,** then it's time to get clever with your spending and saving.

Here are a few ideas:

Payday

When that glorious payday arrives, instead of blowing it all on a ridiculously expensive romantic dinner or some new Italian-made leather goods, try going home and writing some cheques first. Or even better, paying your bills online straight away. This way, the money will already be gone from your account before it can be frittered away on items other than tiresome necessities such as rent, food, mobile phone, and heating. Getting the menacing bills out of the way first is a wonderfully easy way to lift a heavy weight off the remainder of the month.

Splitting up

Breaking up is hard to do, especially when it's between you and your money. Here are some ways to make it all easier.

Having several separate current accounts, each allocated for different types of spending, like groceries and going out, can really help you keep track of your outgoings. It's a bit like cashing your monthly wages and dividing your income into separate, labelled mugs. If you have these accounts with different banks you can also benefit from having several different designs of cards; this makes it easier not to confuse which budgets you are spending.

Allocating a certain percentage – no matter how small – of your monthly wages to a savings account is a pain-free method of watching funds grow, while retaining a separate account for daily ins and outs. If you put aside, for example, 10 per cent of each month's wages to the separate savings account, in a few weeks or months, depending on how generous your wages are, you will have enough saved up for a nice big treat. The trick is keeping the savings money separate and inaccessible enough that you don't find yourself considering it as spending money ...

Another way to split up funds is to have separate wallets. One wallet filled with cash entirely devoted to your monthly cultural activities, or evenings out on the town. When the cash from this wallet runs dry, you're done, and you can feel better knowing exactly how much you've spent on that particular kind of activity that month.

Navigating away from temptation

The old saying, 'never do your grocery shopping on an empty stomach', is true. When you do, you're bound to spend far more money and a week later you're stuck with an ambitious refrigerator bloated with rotting produce and mouldy cheese. Online shopping can alleviate this problem – as long as you're not sitting online in a food-free flat with a belly rumbling like a train.

Most big supermarket chains as well as many organic food stores offer online shopping and handily deliver groceries straight to the doorstep. **Having fully digested a meal beforehand, set to clicking your way through the aisles and adding only the necessities to your virtual cart.** All the while, the website keeps a computed tally of what you've e-chucked into the cart, and those distractingly fancy end-of-the-aisle displays aren't there to lead you into gastronomical temptation. It's an easy, convenient way to save money: no long queues, no (well, minimized) marketing campaigns to steer you away from the bare, inexpensive necessities, and no hauling the groceries in the rain. The delivery fee will usually amount to less than petrol or bus fare.

Other kinds of online shopping are easier on the wallet, too. Those in the market for a particular item, such as a digital camera or a nautical-striped cardigan, are much more likely to get a better deal doing their shopping online. Online searching can also stop you straying into temptation as there are no live vendors, dance music, or racks of pretty tops to help fish out even more money from your account – assuming, of course, that you don't get led astray by those 'click here for more great offers' internet banners.

If after analysing your outgoings you find that an inordinately large percentage of your funds seems to be going towards 'Entertainment Purchases', then you might want to re-think what you're spending on. If, for example, you know your devotion to DVDs borders on addiction, you could promise yourself only to buy them with cash. That way, the psychological tricks that debit cards play with our perception of money can be avoided and you will really be able to see how many pounds you spend on films each month. After a while, the frequent dashes to the cash station to feed your habit will begin to get tiresome – all the better for your savings!

Keeping your balance

Make a habit of knowing how much money is in your account. Recent technology has given us the opportunity to keep an eye on our funds very easily. With banks offering to text your balance through to your mobile and free online banking, you are able to stay atop of your finances painlessly.

Each Monday morning before work, log in and review how much you've spent over the past week and what you have left to play with in the upcoming week. Regularly checking in on your own funds gives you more power over your spending habits and helps to keep wild purchasing at bay. Most importantly, it leaves you in control of your money.

Mmm, pie (charts)

Fancy stationery or colourful financial spreadsheets are a great way to make budgeting seem more enjoyable than it actually is. There is plenty of financial software out there that can really help with your bookkeeping skills. Most illustrate monthly spending behaviour in a fancy pie chart or bar graph, among other tricks. It's worth checking them out, if only to watch how pretty your outgoing payments look as they work themselves out.

While not as delicious as a strawberry rhubarb pie topped with vanilla ice cream on a hot summer's day, pie charts can be pretty useful in terms of figuring out your spending habits.

Labelling your purchases

When you finally apply your carefully hoarded funds to what you've been saving for, help to ease the psychological sting of that newly depleted savings account by labelling how you earned the item/holiday/etc. For instance, it could have come from years of hard work, a famous art collector's commission, or even a lucky find rifling through several long-unused pockets before sticking your clothes in the washing machine. Then, the many years of enjoyment you'll reap as the owner of the longed-for product will have an extra special significance. For example, when breakfast is laid out every morning on your brand new designer kitchen table, you can smile at the thought that you now own it thanks to a most fortuitous laundry day.

Bookkeeping to enlighten your days

Once you have figured out exactly how much money goes into both savings and expenditures each month you can make a reverse calculation and match the amounts up against your wages to see how it balances out with the time you spend working.

For example, let's say you love the theatre, and you take yourself to shows twice a month. If tickets cost around £40, and you make £100 per day at your job, then mark into your calendar that the second Tuesday of every month goes straight into your theatrical obsession. It will make those Tuesday afternoons far more enjoyable if you think of your work as directly enabling you to enjoy your passion for the West End.

This approach could enliven your feelings about your work drastically because you'll know that all those hard-working hours don't simply go towards faceless bills. If on the last Wednesday of every month, all your income goes directly into your pension, then you can smile at your desk on that special Wednesday knowing that you are providing for your old, toothless self to enjoy a relaxing, work-free day in the future.

Future Thinking

Who knows what the future holds? Some cheery souls may chirrup about global warming, the four horsemen of the Apocalypse and a new world order, while others dream of space tourism, virtual reality computer games and a bin that puts itself out on a Thursday night.

Hopefully, financial blue skies will figure somewhere in this future, and once you've extricated yourself from debt, you can start to make your money work for you. Saving is a huge topic – and, in fact, we've even written a book about it, cunningly entitled *Saving*. A few of the possibilities to consider are: investing in property, saving for your retirement or banking ethically. Whatever you choose to do with your money once you've got yourself out of debt and started to have a few quid to spare, that same positive approach that cleared your debts will keep your positive balance growing.

Ethical Banking

Ethical banking is a little bit like when your mum buys your dad a cookery book for Christmas. It's generosity combined with self-interest – having your cake and eating it.

Bank accounts, and particularly those that lock your money away in a savings account, usually involve investments in other companies. Often, if not invariably, these companies make their profit at someone else's expense.

This means that while you might get a fat return on your international bond, some African tribe finds its sworn enemies suddenly wielding cut-price assault rifles; or a South-American rodent peeks out of its burrow one morning to find that the jungle it once lived in has now become a flash, parquet floor in someone's loft apartment. Perhaps we all ought to take an interest in what our money gets up to behind our backs.

What can you do?
It's a pleasant idea that once you've put your own finances in a sustainable position, you can use them, at least in some small way, to do the same out there in the world around you. There are a number of ways you can get that warm inner glow:

Bank with an ethical bank – Some banks have strict ethical policies applying to all their dealings. They may do things like offer free banking to charities and community groups, while refusing to service companies with sketchier records.

Ask your bank if they invest in ethical funds – Companies involved in this will have been given the moral seal of approval by EIRIS (see opposite). As with other bonds, you can get them at varying risk levels. Safer bets will be ones who invest in UK companies, while global bonds tend to be a touch riskier (but sometimes higher paying) because they're linked to foreign economies.

Get an ethical ISA – Since the government doesn't tax you on gains on an ISA, you're already quids in. Ethical ISAs will give you a slightly lower interest rate than some others might, but they will donate a percentage of their profits to carefully vetted charities.

Get a green mortgage – Some of these have policies meaning they will only lend on energy-efficient homes or regeneration projects, while most will give a percentage of the interest that you pay them to charity.

Get an ethical credit card – For those with a regular income who reckon that they can keep tabs on their credit-card spending, an ethical credit card donates a small percentage (usually around 0.25 per cent) of your spending to charity, though they do tend to come with slightly higher interest rates to compensate.

When is a bank ethical?

If you go for an ethical bond, the fund manager will only invest in companies that meet certain criteria. They'll lean towards ventures that champion equal opportunities, community involvement and environmental projects, and will be unlikely to connect your money to alcohol, tobacco, gambling, porn, guns, animal cruelty or tinpot dictators. Independent bodies, such as the Ethical Investment Research Services (EIRIS), give out seals of approval and rate companies against strict criteria, including governance, social responsibilities and any specific ethical concerns.

Of course, it isn't as simple as that

When you talk about ethical banking, some financial experts will laugh, and tell you it doesn't exist. Sooner or later if you trace every penny through investors, employees, customers and beyond (it's a tangled web) you're bound to find something dubious.

Also, some would argue that accounts and mortgages where the bank gives a percentage to charity are not as practical as they might seem. Generally lower interest rates on these accounts mean that you could be better off investing in a higher rate (or lower rate, in the case of a mortgage) account, and giving what you make or save to charity yourself.

For more information on the subject visit the following websites:

→ **www.ethicaljunction.org** – Details about general ethical living, including a finance section.

→ **www.foe.co.uk** – The Friends of the Earth have a section on ethical investment.

→ **www.co-operativebank.co.uk** – The Co-op has been banking ethically since 1992.

→ **www.smile.co.uk** – The internet-based subsidiary of the Co-operative Bank.

→ **www.activatemoney.com** – Triodos bank specializes in environmentally ethical saving.

→ **www.eiris.org** – The Ethical Investment Research Services.

Mortgages

A mortgage is simply an enormous, secured loan, paid back over a very long period of time, and at the end of it, providing you pay it all off, you'll own a property.

As long as houses hold their value, mortgage lenders will hand over huge sums of cash in order for you to snap up the pad of your fantasies so that the loan is secured. If you don't pay up then they reserve the right to sell your home in order to pay off the debt. Given that you're less likely to default on this sort of loan than on, say, a credit-card bill, the risk to the lender is much lower.

The amount you can get depends on your income, how big a deposit you can find and various other crafty formulae that the lenders have in place to work out what sort of risk they think you are.

It sounds rather fine to own your own place, but a mortgage isn't something to be taken on lightly. Property markets are notorious for making people very rich on the upswing and very poor when they crash. With the risk of prices falling or interest rates being hiked up, being a homeowner can be a precarious activity. On the other hand – depending on where you live – rent can cost as much as a mortgage repayment and you will have nothing to show for it at the end.

Of the vast range of mortgage products out there, most can be divided into two categories: repayment mortgages and interest-only mortgages. Repayment is where the money you hand over each month makes inroads into paying off the main body of the loan, while interest-only, astonishingly enough, means you only pay off the interest that's accruing on the amount.

Repayment mortgages mean larger monthly bills, but at the end of the 25 years (or however long the term is – and they are getting longer all the time), providing you keep up the repayments, you'll own your home. With an interest-only mortgage, you would use the spare cash to make investments with which you could pay the basic value of the loan off at the end, or you would simply sell the place to pay the sum – fingers crossed you get enough for the property when you sell, otherwise you'll be left owing the bank.

If you do decide to take the plunge, then the world, his wife and her sister will be wanting to sell you their own very special mortgage. Mortgages are a complicated business, and what you need is an independent mortgage broker. There are lots of helpful avenues for advice out there, and searching around could save you a pile of cash in the long run.

If the risks seem too high, there's absolutely nothing wrong with renting – as long as you are putting money away somewhere for the future. A lot of people approach a mortgage like a pension (see page 86), planning on selling their home when they retire, buying somewhere smaller and living off the money left over. However, this relies on the property prices remaining high.

→ **www.moneysavingexpert.com/mortgages/mortgage-guide** – A good introduction to mortgages by Martin Lewis.

→ **www.en.wikipedia.org/wiki/UK_mortgage_terminology** – Useful jargon-busting Wikipedia article on the different kinds of interest.

→ **www.moneymadeclear.fsa.gov.uk** – On the FSA website you can find a mortgage calculator and see what type of mortgage you might need and how much you could end up paying back.

Pensions

Chances are some day you will be sitting in a rocking chair, living a futuristic life of leisure and telling lies to your grandchildren about how you remember when all the houses around you were just fields.

It would be nice if, at this ripe old age, you could be comfortable and devote yourself to such heady pursuits as ballroom dancing or model railways, rather than to topping up the milk with water and burning your rocking chair for warmth in winter.

When you retire, you'll need a steady source of income to replace your salary. Your outgoings may have fallen, since you will probably no longer have children to support or mortgages to pay off, but there'll still be things to finance. This is where a pension comes in.

A pension is a way of saving for old age, and it's a more effective way than most, since you get loads of tax breaks on it. State pensions are paid from your National Insurance contributions. The amount is not generous, but it's definitely better than nothing.

A lot of employers have company pension schemes, and if yours does then it's worth getting in on the action as swiftly as possible. Not only does the government supplement your contributions, but so does your employer, meaning that the money grows faster than in just about any other type of account.

If your company doesn't have one of these, then it's a good idea to look into getting a personal pension, and they will also often let you take part of the fund as a tax-free lump sum.

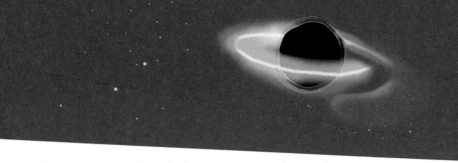

Obviously it won't benefit from the company's contributions, but in a bid to make people save more for their old age, the government offer some very generous tax breaks that mean you still end up getting a good return on your money. At the time of writing the government was giving tax back to pension schemes at a rate of 22 per cent, effectively meaning that every £78 you pay in becomes £100.

→ **www.thepensionservice.gov.uk/** – Just what it says.

→ **www.direct.gov.uk/en/MoneyTaxAndBenefits/Pensions AndRetirement/index.htm** – Advice on and explanation of pensions and retirement plans.

When to start paying into a pension

It's never too soon to start saving for your retirement, and the younger you start, the smaller the payments you will need to make to save the same amount. Money paid into a pension scheme does not vanish into the ether never to be seen again. When all's said and done, it's still yours, although you can't just cash in a pension should you suddenly need a lump sum: there are age restrictions and limits on amounts, plus there may also be cash penalties. A pension is the wrong place to put money that you may need to get your hands on in a hurry.

If you don't make it to pensionable age, the amount in the fund goes to your nearest and dearest, the same as everything else you own. It's worth knowing that this doesn't necessarily apply to company pensions, as it depends what kind of scheme an individual company operates.

Glossary

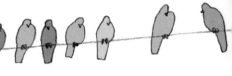

Administration order A court order whereby you make regular payments, which the court then distributes amongst your creditors. Your creditors have to leave you alone while this is happening, but the court will take its own cut.

Bailiff A person, registered or unregistered, who comes on behalf of your creditors to take your stuff and sell it at auction. Proceeds of such sales go towards paying off your debts.

AER (Annual Effective Rate) The amount of interest you'd earn per year, taking into account how often interest is added.

APR (Annual Percentage Rate) The amount of interest you will pay on a loan per year; it can be used to work out the total cost of taking out a loan, including administrative costs and other hidden extras.

BACS payments Bankers Automated Clearing Services. A way of moving money electronically from one account to another, and the method by which most employers pay their staff.

Balance The amount of money in an account. This can be either a positive balance, if you have money in the account, or a negative balance, if you owe money (i.e. an overdraft).

Balance transfer The act of moving a balance, either positive or negative, between accounts, such as when you take out a new credit card and move your debt from the old card to the new one.

Bankruptcy A way of liquidating all your assets to settle all your outstanding debts. A way of finding a fresh start, but at a very big price.

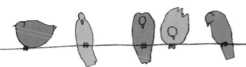

Bankruptcy restriction orders
A list of things you are not
allowed to do within an allotted
time period if you have been
bankrupt.

Bursary An amount of money
set aside by a university to help
fund the education of particularly clever or financially needy
students.

Beer The codename for a gaping
yet invisible hole in the side of
your wallet out of which money
mysteriously escapes.

Bond A high-interest account
that locks your money away for
a while. Worth considering if
you have any spare cash you're
fairly certain you won't need for
a while. The returns are usually
higher than a standard savings
account.

Budgeting Making the numbers
work. Basically what people mean
when they say you have got to
make sure you have more money
coming in than going out.

Capped interest An interest rate
that is fixed so it can't rise above
a specified amount.

Career development loan
A way of financing a postgraduate degree or other further
education course.

**CCCS (Consumer Credit
Counselling Service)** A charity
which offers free advice for
people in debt.

CCJ (County Court Judgment)
When a court orders you to pay
money, for whatever reason,
it goes on a register. If you pay
promptly, you can get the entry
in the register cancelled,
otherwise it will stay there for six
years, and will be visible to anyone assessing your credit rating.

Compound interest The interest paid on the loan itself as well as on the unpaid interest on the loan.

Consolidation loan One big old loan that you take out to pay off lots of smaller ones. This can save you both time and money, as interest rates on bank loans are usually friendlier than those on credit cards.

Credit limit The cap on how much credit you can obtain on a particular card.

Credit rating A measure of how much credit a lender will give you. It's based on a number of criteria, for example, your presence on the electoral roll and how reliable you have been at paying your debts. Your credit rating can also affect the interest rate you are charged on a loan.

CRAs (Credit Reference Agencies) Agencies who provide potential lenders with information about your credit history. The big names are Experian, Equifax and Callcredit.

Credit card A plastic card that allows you to spend money you don't yet have by borrowing it from a company and repaying it through monthly bills – with very high interest rates. One of the most effective ways of getting into debt scarily quickly.

Debit card A piece of plastic that allows you to spend and withdraw money from your account (including any available overdraft).

Debt counsellor Someone who can advise you about dealing with problem debts. Some counsellors are free (see page 58), while others are naked profiteers who will charge you generously for their time and try to sell you inappropriate financial products.

Debt management plan A plan for controlling and solving debt, usually devised by a debt-counselling organization.

Defenestration A great word meaning to throw something or someone out of a window. Totally irrelevant to financial matters, but a good one to throw into an embarrassingly flagging conver sation.

Hardship fund Financial aid given by universities to students who find themselves with serious and unexpected money troubles.

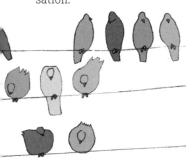

Ethical banking Investing your money in an ethical manner. This could be through getting a credit card that donates a percentage of the interest to charity, investing in funds that are not tied to shady industries, or simply popping your wages in an account with an ethical bank.

FSA The Financial Services Authority, which regulates all businesses selling financial products.

IFAs (Independent Financial Advisers) Financial advisers who are not affiliated to a company. This means they will generally give you more impartial advice because they will be choosing from a much wider range of financial products than an affiliated financial adviser, who will only recommend the products that their particular firm offers.

Inflation The changing value of currency, or 'why everything is more expensive than it used to be'.

Insolvency When the numbers don't work.

Interim order A court order which stops your creditors pursuing a bankruptcy petition against you, usually while you are resolving an IVA.

Interest The money that lenders charge you for the privilege of borrowing from them.

Interest-free period A pleasing introductory offer where credit-card providers don't charge you interest for the first few months after taking out a card with them.

Interest-only mortgage A mortgage where you only pay off the interest that is accruing on the loan, and the original amount borrowed remains untouched.

Interest rate The fee taken by a lender in exchange for giving you a loan. This is usually expressed as a percentage of the total amount which you have to pay back on top of what you originally borrowed.

ISA An account that allows you to save a certain amount of money tax free each year.

IVA (Individual Voluntary Arrangement) An increasingly popular alternative to bankruptcy.

Loyalty card A way of getting rewards points for spending money in particular shops. You gain points; they gain lots of data about you and your spending habits.

Maintenance loan One element of a student loan. This part of the loan is to cover your living costs, while the other part covers your tuition fees.

Mortgage An enormous loan that you take out in order to buy a property, and pay back over a long period of time.

National Debtline A debt relief charity offering free and reliable advice on digging yourself out of trouble.

Pension The money you save to keep you in your dotage, either through the state, your company, or a personal plan.

Nelson A great name for a spaniel.

Notice of Disassociation A form that you can download from the Credit Reference Agencies websites. It resolves problems that arise from having your name financially linked to someone with a bad credit score.

OFT (Office of Fair Trading) Financial services are products, just like a Ferrari or a tin of beans. If you feel you have been misled or the product was substandard then you can complain to the Office of Fair Trading.

Overdraft The facility that allows you to spend more money than there is in your bank account.

Repayment mortgage Where you repay the entirety of the mortgage plus all the interest that it has accumulated, usually over a term of 25 years.

RPI (Retail Prices Index) A way of measuring inflation, or the decreasing value of money. Many interest rates are linked to the RPI.

Secured loan A loan where you put up something big as collateral; usually a house. Interest rates for secured loans are much better than those for unsecured ones, as lenders will view you as more of a sure thing.

Standing orders An arrangement by which money is debited automatically from your account on a regular basis.

Store card Like a credit card, but you can only use it in certain shops. Treat with care.

Student loan A special loan available to undergraduates to help them meet their tuition fees and living costs; charged at much lower rates than other loans.

Walking possession An agreement whereby things in your home earmarked by a bailiff now legally belong to them. They can come and take them away to sell at any point, but until that time arrives you can still use them to watch *Hollyoaks*/play FIFA/email your creditors and beg them to leave you alone.

Sub-prime lenders Companies who will give loans to people with very low credit scores. They're a bit of a last resort as, due to the added risk, their interest rates are usually rather higher than mainstream lenders.

Unsecured loan A loan that you take out without putting anything up as collateral. The interest rates are not generally as good as secured loans.

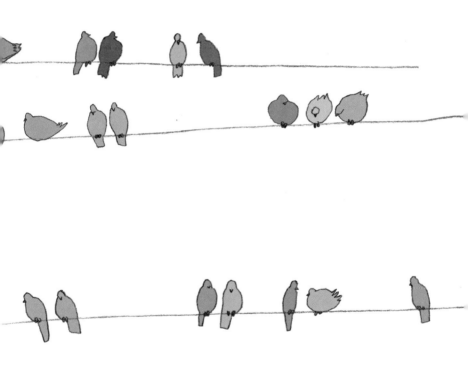

Acknowledgements

One name goes on the cover, but a book is always a team effort, especially this one. I am very grateful for the support that I have received from the lovely people around me. I owe special thanks to Caroline Blake and Matthias Megyeri, who both were absolutely indispensable in the development of the White Rabbit series. They generously helped from day one and have been patrons to the project ever since. I also want to thank Eve Peasnall, who was a great sounding board when we started writing and who helped define the tone of the book.

Furthermore, I want to thank the following people, who all contributed to the success of this publication: Claire Andrews, Marloes ten Böhmer, Gavin O'Carroll, Jane ní Dhulchaointigh, Bryony Fox, Henry Herkner, David Inman, Alex Marshall, Briony Marshall, Hannah Martin, Emma Neuberg, Barbara Otterbach, Carolin Otterbach, Christiane Otterbach, Ulrich Otterbach, Andrew Perkins, Paula Saunders, Zoe Stanton, Clare Tomlinson and Kelly Thompson.

When the White Rabbit series was still at idea stage, Otterbach & Partners was granted an award by the National Endowment for Science, Technology and the Arts (NESTA). Through NESTA's support, in particular Hugo Manassei, Siân Prime, Mark Fenwick and Mark Elliott, we were able to develop this new series.

Credit Action kindly agreed to read through the book and check whether any factual mistakes had sneaked in. Credit Action is a national money-education charity. Their aim is to help people to have better thinking about money, credit, budgeting and debt.